Lemon Moms
COMPANION WORKBOOK

Action Steps to Understand and Survive

Maternal Narcissism

Diane Metcalf

For more information, email Diane@DianeMetcalf.com

Cover design by Diane Metcalf and Christos Angelidakis.

ISBN: 978-1-7352876-2-1

Contents

THE BEGINNING

This workbook prepares you for healing.

You see, to really heal, entirely and for good, you must remember and, to some degree, re-experience your trauma. You'll do this as an adult this time so that you can understand it on an adult level.

To heal, you must take this understanding and validate how someone else's narcissism affected you. You'll reframe those experiences now, as an adult, and move forward.

This workbook is a private and personal space only for you; it's for your eyes only. It's your safe place to reflect upon your reading, learning, thinking, and feeling. No one is going to read, judge, or grade your workbook. Use it to write what's in your heart. Its purpose is to help you work through the more challenging aspects of creating awareness, in a safe emotional space where healing can truly begin.

While it's overwhelming to figure out how to begin the recovery process, I suggest that you keep an open mind, do your research, and experiment to see what works best for you.

Let yourself grieve the loss of the childhood and mother you never got to have. Be kind to yourself.

You'll have good days and not-so-good ones. I can tell you from experience that you'll want to give up at times. You might feel you aren't making progress, or that it's not worth it because it's painful and difficult. Hang in there and keep moving forward.

Chapter One

WHAT IS NARCISSISM?

BOOK CHAPTER REVIEW

- A "false face" is a coping mechanism formed during childhood. It changes and adapts over time, acting as a shield against pain and narcissistic injury.

- Narcissists display personality traits, such as selfishness, vanity, manipulation, and self-importance. They're often defensive, condescending, and "know everything." They can be aggressive and even physically abusive and are challenging when interacting with them.

- Most narcissists will never know whether they're on the NPD spectrum or have full-blown NPD because they don't seek treatment.

"Narcissists lack the ability to emotionally tune in to other people. They cannot feel and show empathy or unconditional love. They are typically critical and judgmental."

—Karyl McBride

NOTES:

The first step in healing is acknowledging that you grew up in a dysfunctional family. You may be reluctant to do this because it's painful, and it stirs up memories that you'd rather keep buried. If these statements are true for you, I encourage you to go at your own pace, making notes and giving yourself time and space for self-reflection for beginning the healing process.

1. Do any of the NPD behaviors and personality traits feel familiar to you? Write about this. Describe the behaviors and traits you've witnessed. As you write, stay aware of your emotions and how you're feeling. Make a note of your feelings as they come: Are you feeling surprised? Shocked? Unsure? Defensive? Sad? Angry? In denial? Describe each emotion you feel.

2. Using what you wrote, focus less on what your mother said or did, and more on how you felt about it. If you can remember, make a list of the feelings you were experiencing at the time. Are your feelings about these experiences different today? Write about that.

_____

_____

_____

_____

_____

_____

_____

_____

3. Look over everything you wrote. Acknowledge that you felt those emotions and that *you had the right to feel them*. Say it aloud: "I felt ___ and ___, and ___ and I had reason to feel those emotions. I lived with this. I witnessed this. It was real."

You are validating *yourself* when you acknowledge your feelings. You are *acknowledging* the fact that you were x years old with big, scary feelings that you may not have known the words for. You were probably confused. If you couldn't tell anyone about these feelings or what was causing them, you probably felt like you had no choice but to keep them bottled up inside. You may have re-experienced these same feelings at other times in your life when you found yourself in similar situations. Let yourself cry if you feel like it. It's OK to feel your feelings. You're in a safe space.

Chapter Two
CREATING A NARCISSIST

- Narcissism often begins in early childhood as a result of trauma caused by a narcissistic parent or caregiver. The "false face" is a coping mechanism that was formed during that time.

- Some kids deal with the trauma by imitating their narcissist caretaker and becoming a narcissist as a result or by pleasing and placating and becoming codependent.

- Kids are vulnerable to becoming targets of narcissistic abuse.

- Narcissistic parents are oblivious to the damage they inflict on their children.

If your mother has been diagnosed with NPD or has NPD characteristics, she may have created a false self during childhood. She protects that false image fiercely because it's everything that her true self is not. From her perspective, the false self is preferable to the real self. The true self is "lacking;" the false self is not. To survive emotionally, she would use the false self to hide and protect her true self.

NOTES:

HEALING STEPS

1. How do you feel when you realize your mother might have been a narcissist's target when she was a child?

_____

_____

_____

_____

_____

_____

_____

2. Are you surprised? Why or why not?

_____

_____

_____

_____

_____

_____

_____

3. Do you feel sad or angry? Why or why not? What else do you feel? Come back to this page and continue writing as you work through this chapter.

_____

_____

_____

_____

_____

_____

_____

4. If your mother was a narcissist's target, could that explain her current way of behaving and relating to you now? Why or why not? What do you know about her childhood? Write about it.

Chapter Three
DIAGNOSTIC CRITERIA

- In the DSM-5, there are nine criteria for diagnosing narcissistic personality disorder. All emphasize feeling superior, having arrogant behavior, and beliefs of being entitled or special.

- To be diagnosed with narcissistic personality disorder, at least five of these traits need to be expressed.

- Narcissists demand attention and admiration, lack empathy, take advantage, and hold a high amount of contempt for others.

- When someone has NPD, they display a limited behavior pattern that repeats itself, regardless of your reaction or response.

Having a personality disorder or being on the narcissism spectrum doesn't mean a narcissist is a "bad" person, but it does significantly decrease their ability to have mutually satisfying relationships.

NOTES:

HEALING STEPS

1. After reading this chapter, list the things that you learned about narcissism that you didn't know before.

2. Have you observed any characteristics of narcissism in your mother? What are they? Do you think she is aware of these characteristics? Has she ever sought therapy or treatment? If so, what prompted it? What kind? How long? What changes, if any, did you see as a result?

_____

_____

_____

_____

_____

_____

_____

_____

_____

_____

3. How has what you've learned so far impacted your thoughts or feelings about your childhood? This is a tough question. You may feel angry, confused, guilty, frustrated, even hatred, among other feelings. Let yourself feel what you feel without judgment. Validate and accept your feelings.

_____

_____

_____

_____

_____

_____

_____

_____

_____

4. Look over what you wrote. Acknowledge what you feel. Say aloud, "I feel ___, and ___, and ___."

You are validating *yourself* when you do this. You are *acknowledging* the fact that you feel these feelings and that it's OK to explore them. Feelings come and go. They intensify, and then they wane. Although it's hard, sit with these feelings and remind yourself that you are a human being who is supposed to feel and experience emotions. Acknowledge that feeling is a part of life.

5. Acknowledge that you might be feeling unforgiving, or like wanting to talk with a counselor or support group. You may want to rediscover yourself or begin to take better care of yourself. How do you feel about doing these things?

_____

_____

_____

_____

_____

_____

_____

_____

_____

_____

6. Hold yourself. Cry if you want to. Envision the little child that you were back then and talk to them. Tell them that you're here for them now. Let them know that you've learned some things you didn't know before and that they were never to blame for what happened. Tell them that they were always worthy and always good enough. Promise them you'll continue learning and growing and changing and that they'll never have to endure that kind of treatment again. Sooth them and love them the way they should have been loved. This is called "inner child work." If this kind of healing work speaks to you, I think you should pursue it. There are many free resources online that can help with inner-child healing work. Continue writing your thoughts and feelings.

_____

_____

_____

_____

_____

_____

_____

_____

_____

_____

Chapter Four
TYPES OF NARCISSISM

- There are two main types of narcissism: grandiose and vulnerable

- There are two subtypes: overt vs. covert.

- A narcissist mom usually reveals her true self during a time of crisis, conflict, or high stress.

- Acquaintances, friends, and extended family of a narcissist mom often don't see the false face for what it is.

- Children of narcissists have a hard time getting people to understand or believe what's going on at home.

Narcissists don't feel a sense of remorse or conscience. They believe that everything they do is justified or is someone else's fault. They don't take responsibility for their actions, which makes them unable to feel guilt. To feel guilty, it's necessary to feel empathy and remorse.

NOTES:

HEALING STEPS

1. If you had/have a mother (caretaker/mother figure) who showed symptoms of narcissism, talk about the possible type of narcissism you think it could have been and include its probable subtype. Give examples that support your thought process.

_____

_____

_____

_____

_____

_____

_____

_____

_____

2. Write the insights or "aha" moments you had while reading this chapter.

3. Those of us who've discovered we've been negatively affected by our mother's narcissism often feel sad and experience symptoms of grief. Write about how you feel concerning the effects your mother's narcissism has had on you.

_____

_____

_____

_____

_____

_____

_____

_____

_____

_____

_____

4. Have you experienced triangulation? Write about it. Who was in the triangle? How did you handle it? What will be different about the way you handle it next time?

5. Has your mother ever excluded you? Write about that: where it happened, who was there, how it made you feel. Include how you'll deal with it the next time it happens.

_____

_____

_____

_____

_____

_____

_____

_____

_____

_____

_____

_____

_____

_____

_____

_____

_____

_____

_____

_____

_____

_____

_____

_____

_____

_____

_____

_____

_____

_____

Chapter Five

THE TRAUMATIZED BRAIN

BOOK CHAPTER REVIEW

- The amygdala's job is to convert and move information from short-term memory to long-term memory and to connect emotions to these memories. The amygdala gives meaning and a degree of emotional intensity to the memory.

- The hippocampus continues to be the focus of research regarding cognition (understanding through thought, experience, and senses) and memory-retention in post-traumatic stress disorder (PTSD).

- Traumatic memories are stored as bits of visual images, smells, sounds, tastes, or physical contact.

- When emotions aren't self-regulated, we continue to respond to old, buried memories with an automatic, knee-jerk behavior called "triggering."

- C-PTSD results from a series of trauma-causing events, or one prolonged event. Children who experience neglect or ongoing traumatic abuse are at risk of developing complex C-PTSD.

"There are wounds that never show on the body that are deeper and more hurtful than anything that bleeds."

—Laurell K. Hamilton, *Mistral's Kiss*

NOTES:

1. What is the first traumatic memory that comes to mind? In as much detail as you care to, describe it and others here. Include those experiences that still leave you feeling hurt or confused today. Describe them the way you remember them happening, not the way you may have been told they happened.

2. Do you have triggers? As you discover them, write about them here. Include your thoughts about where each trigger came from and how you handle each of them currently. For example: What triggers instant anger? When someone says or does something that angers you, what was the first thing you felt or *thought* that ignited the anger? Maybe your first thought was, "They're saying I don't matter!" Could that thought have been a misinterpretation? A conclusion you jumped to? Do you see how you could be triggered because you have unhealed hurts or faulty beliefs that you still need to address? How do you plan to work on your triggers? Using the example above, you could start by recognizing that you've been triggered, and maybe even stop and say you've been triggered, then remove yourself from the situation. Take a look at those first moments of anger and what your first thoughts were. See where they came from in your past. Sometimes all it takes is to realize that we're dealing with an old unhealed hurt that has no relevance in the current interaction.

_____

_____

_____

_____

_____

_____

_____

_____

3. No matter who triggers you, or how it happens, your triggers are your responsibility to understand and heal.

_____

_____

_____

_____

_____

_____

_____

_____

_____

_____

4. As you continue your healing process, make it a priority to become aware of new triggers. Give examples of how each new trigger has shown up in your life. Include a plan for how you will handle each of them when they appear again.

5. Give a recent example of becoming triggered. What does it trace back to? Think about the ways you can respond differently the next time this particular trigger comes up.

_____

_____

_____

_____

_____

_____

_____

_____

_____

_____

_____

_____

_____

_____

_____

_____

_____

_____

_____

_____

_____

_____

_____

_____

_____

_____

_____

_____

Chapter Six

LOOKING BACK: OUR PAST

BOOK CHAPTER REVIEW

- Growing up in a toxic or neglectful environment can create problems that can last a lifetime.

- Childhood trauma physically changes the brain and negatively impacts the way it functions.

- The act of validating is an essential aspect of parenting because it establishes a feeling of safety.

- Trust is a cornerstone of every relationship, especially between mothers and their children, because of their unique relationship.

- Validation requires empathy; therefore, a narcissistic mother will not be able to perform this responsibility.

- One of the keys to healing from toxicity and developing healthy coping skills is to acknowledge our codependency and to begin to recover from it.

"The conflict between the will to deny horrible events and the will to proclaim them aloud is the central dialectic of psychological trauma."

—Judith Lewis Herman

NOTES:

1. Think of ways that your mother validated you while you were growing up. Did she listen when you spoke? Did she acknowledge how you felt? Did she dismiss you or tell you that you shouldn't feel the way you did? Did she accept your memories "as is," or did she want you to remember certain events differently? Validate your memories here by writing in detail about them.

2. Were you a "helper" as a child? Did you like to jump in a do things for others, even when they could do it for themselves? Did you often look for ways to help? Were you often "there" for others? Give examples of ways that you've helped or tried to fix other's problems. Why do you think you needed to help? Was it expected? Did it give you a sense of self-esteem or purpose? Explore those questions here:

_____

_____

_____

_____

_____

_____

_____

_____

Chapter Seven
NARCISSISM AWARENESS GRIEF

BOOK CHAPTER REVIEW

- Narcissistic Grief Awareness happens when we become aware of our mother's narcissism and begin to realize how it impacted us.

- There are six phases to work through in narcissistic grief awareness.

- The phases are not experienced in any particular order, and it's possible to become stuck in one and not progress forward without some assistance.

- We can't get to the final phase of acceptance without working through the previous five stages.

"Your mother doesn't need a diagnosis for you to determine that
your relationship with her is unhealthy."

NOTES:

Healing Steps

1. Write at length about the feelings you're experiencing as you enter the phases of narcissistic awareness grief. Make a section just for writing about your feelings of grief.

2. Include these topics:

Denial: How does it feel when you think of your mother as a narcissist?

_____

_____

_____

_____

_____

_____

_____

_____

3. Is it important for you to protect your mother's image? Is it more important to protect your mother than to face some uncomfortable truths about her or yourself? Explain.

Continue writing about your feelings of:

4. Betrayal

_____

_____

_____

_____

_____

_____

_____

_____

5. Confusion

_____

_____

_____

_____

_____

_____

_____

_____

6. Rejection

_____

_____

_____

_____

_____

_____

_____

_____

7. Shame

_____

_____

_____

_____

_____

_____

_____

_____

8. Anger

_____

_____

_____

_____

_____

_____

_____

_____

_____

9. Fear: What are you afraid of? Give a best-and worst-case scenario for each thing. Does it decrease your fear when you do this exercise? Why or why not?

_____

_____

_____

_____

_____

_____

_____

_____

10. Abandonment

11. Loneliness and isolation: Talk about how these feel. Can you think of ways to feel reconnected?

_____

_____

_____

_____

_____

_____

12. Write about other feelings you're dealing with.

_____

_____

_____

_____

_____

_____

_____

Chapter Eight

THE NARCISSISTIC MOTHER

BOOK CHAPTER REVIEW

- A narcissistic mother sees her kids as extensions of herself, and because of that, to her, everything the kids do and say reflects on *her*.

- When a narcissistic mother doesn't like aspects of her own personality, she emotionally separates herself from those qualities and then "projects" those unacceptable traits onto one or more of her children.

- A narcissistic mother can emotionally hurt or injure her children in a variety of ways.

"The eyes see only what the mind is prepared to comprehend."

–Henri Bergson

NOTES:

HEALING STEPS

1. Have you been a target of projection? In what way has your mother used projection to see her own unacceptable traits within you?

_____

_____

_____

_____

_____

_____

_____

_____

_____

2. Do you think you've been intentionally hurt by your mother? Explain.

3. The first step in healing is acknowledging that you grew up in a dysfunctional family. You may be reluctant to do this because it may feel painful or shameful. It may stir up painful memories that you'd rather keep buried. If these statements are true for you, I encourage you to go at your own pace and give yourself time and space for self-reflection and beginning the grieving process.

_____

_____

_____

_____

_____

_____

_____

_____

_____

_____

4. You may be feeling denial, fear, confusion, shame, rejection, loneliness, abandonment, or any number and combination of emotions. These feelings are all an expected part of acknowledging what's happened, and to begin the grieving process. Write about your feelings.

Chapter Nine

THE NARCISSISTIC ABUSE CYCLE

BOOK CHAPTER REVIEW

- The abuse cycle defined by Dr. Walker has four stages: Tension Building, Abusive Incident, Remorsefulness, and the Honeymoon Phase. The cycle will continuously repeat until either the abuser or the target change their way of interacting.

- In the narcissistic abuse cycle, the roles in the "Remorsefulness" stage get reversed. A narcissist-mom will play the part of the victim, and the mistreated child/children will appease and apologize.

- There's a particularly dysfunctional family dynamic where family members are assigned roles of the Golden Child, Invisible Child, and Scapegoat. Any part can be attributed to any child at any time by the mother.

"Narcissistic mothers revel in generating competition between their children and emotionally distancing them from one another."

NOTES:

Using Dr. Christine Hammonds "Cycle of Narcissistic Abuse" diagram, answer the following questions:

1. Narcissistic
   Injury

2. Abusive
   Incident

4. Narcissist
   Empowered

3. Role
   Reversal

1. Have you witnessed the narcissistic abuse cycle in your own family? If so, in which stage is the family currently? Observe and monitor the cycle. What have you noticed? Using what you've learned so far, what do you think will happen next?

_____

_____

_____

_____

_____

_____

2. Do you see the Golden, Invisible, and Scapegoat roles played in your family? What role are you currently in? What other roles have you played? Give examples.

_____

_____

_____

_____

_____

_____

3. How can you stop feeling like a victim in these family dynamics? Take steps to look for a counselor or support group, where you can safely share your thoughts and emotions and learn how.

Chapter Ten

NARCISSISTIC LYING

BOOK CHAPTER REVIEW

- All human beings lie. Our reasons and motives for lying and the types of lies we tell are all as different as the people who tell them.

- A narcissistic mother's lies are a combination of her character and life experiences, so there's usually a small kernel of truth in each lie.

- Narcissists need to believe they're always correct, that they never make mistakes, so they often have a hard time telling the difference between their own lies and the truth.

- Narcissistic behaviors, including lying, are unconsciously motivated by shame and driven by previous narcissistic injuries.

"Narcissistic behaviors, including lying, are unconsciously motivated by shame and driven by previous narcissistic injuries."

NOTES:

Healing Steps

The more you learn about the impact of maternal narcissism on your life, the more you may want to deny that you were a target of such behavior. Continue writing about your feelings and discoveries. Write about your childhood family dynamics, as well as your relationship with your mom.

1. Have you ever lied? What kind of lie was it? What was your motivation? Who or what (for example, a relationship) did the lie hurt?

_____

_____

_____

_____

_____

_____

_____

_____

_____

_____

2. Has your mother ever lied to you? What kind of lie was it? What do you think her motivation was? Whom or what did it hurt?

_____

_____

_____

_____

_____

_____

_____

_____

_____

_____

_____

3. Do you still believe the lie? Why or why not? What else can you choose to believe instead?

Chapter Eleven

THE SILENT TREATMENT

BOOK CHAPTER REVIEW

- Narcissistic moms love the silent treatment, and it's their secret weapon when they want to manipulate and hurt.

- A narcissistic mother gets her sense of self through her children. Her children are a necessary part of her identity.

- The silent treatment is a "hurt and rescue" type of cycle. It's meant to keep us anxious by triggering our fear of abandonment.

- When we're actively ignored, it causes such psychological and emotional anguish that it can actually be seen on brain scans.

- Trauma bonding occurs when two people become deeply connected by going through cycles of abuse together.

"The silent treatment is a punishment that consists of a "hurt and rescue" cycle."

NOTES:

HEALING STEPS

1. Have you experienced the silent treatment? By whom?

_____

_____

_____

_____

_____

_____

_____

_____

_____

2. Write specifically about this event:

Who stopped speaking to you? Why? How did you feel about it? How long did it last? How was the silent treatment ended? How would you handle it differently if it happens again?

_____

_____

_____

_____

_____

_____

_____

_____

_____

_____

_____

3. Have trusting, open conversations with your therapist, a trusted friend, or a support group about your childhood memories. Determine to let go of the dysfunctional family rules of "Don't Talk, Don't Trust, Don't Feel." Silence keeps the issues hidden and doesn't benefit anybody. How do you feel about the dysfunctional family rules? Does your family follow them?

Chapter Twelve
SHAME

BOOK CHAPTER REVIEW

- A narcissist mother shames her children in a multitude of ways.

- You may intentionally minimize your painful childhood experiences because you don't want to think of your mothers as an "abuser" or yourself as a target of abuse.

- A mixed message is a type of communication where the narcissist communicates by giving conflicting information.

- You may intentionally minimize your painful childhood experiences because you don't want to think of your mothers as an "abuser" or yourself as a target of abuse.

- Shaming her children allows a narcissistic mother to feel superior and minimizes future threats, like embarrassing comments they may make about her.

"Shame is the intensely painful feeling or experience of believing we are flawed and therefore unworthy of acceptance and belonging."

—*Brené Brown*

NOTES:

HEALING STEPS

1. Have you experienced feelings of shame? When did it start? Are you still ashamed? What are you ashamed of?

_____

_____

_____

_____

_____

_____

2. In looking at these incidents with a fresh perspective, how do you think about and understand them now? Are you still ashamed? Why or why not?

3. Do you feel ready to forgive? Even if you're not, I suggest being open to the possibility. Read about forgiveness and learn how it would benefit you. Remember, the benefits of forgiveness are for you, not your mother.

_____

_____

_____

_____

_____

_____

4. If you haven't reached out to a counselor or support group, now would be a great time to pursue that. Some counselors offer a sliding-fee scale, meaning that you pay what you can afford according to your income. Do you plan to look for a mental health professional? Keep track of your contacts here. Include name, type of service, email, phone number, date contacted, the fees for service, and personal comments/notes.

5. Read Brené Brown's books on vulnerability and shame:

- "I Thought It Was Just Me (But It Isn't)—Making the Journey from 'What Will People Think' to 'I Am Enough'"

- "The Power of Vulnerability: Teachings of Authenticity, Connection, and Courage"

Ms. Brown also has two excellent TED talks on the topics of vulnerability and shame:

- The Power of Vulnerability:

  ted.com/talks/brene_brown_the_power_of_vulnerability

- Listening to Shame:

  ted.com/talks/brene_brown_listening_to_shame

Chapter Thirteen
NARCISSISTIC SUPPLY

- Narcissistic supply is the admiration a narcissist needs to feel to keep their self-esteem intact. They take this admiration and support from the people in their environment.

- A narcissistic mom cannot survive without narcissistic supply, which is like emotional food. Any emotional reaction, positive or negative, we give a narcissistic mother can be a form of supply.

- Acquaintances, friends, and extended family often don't see the narcissism for what it is.

- A narcissistic mom usually reveals her true self during a time of crisis, conflict, or high stress.

"What you allow is what will continue."

—Unknown

NOTES:

1. Have you been a source of narcissistic supply? How? Write about it.

_____

_____

_____

_____

_____

_____

_____

_____

_____

2. How will you change that, now that you're aware of the dynamic?

3. What, if anything, has contributed to your becoming a source of supply?

_____

_____

_____

_____

_____

_____

_____

_____

_____

_____

_____

_____

_____

_____

_____

_____

_____

_____

_____

_____

_____

_____

_____

_____

_____

_____

_____

_____

_____

_____

_____

_____

Chapter Fourteen
TRAUMA BONDING

BOOK CHAPTER REVIEW

- Trauma bonding is a survival tool where the abused becomes emotionally attached to the abuser and will justify, side with, and defend them.

- Trauma bonding with a narcissistic mother makes future trauma bonding likely.

- In a healthy relationship, there is no trauma bonding.

- Trauma bonding can keep us stuck in codependency. The first step to breaking a trauma bond is becoming aware that one exists.

- "Adverse Childhood Experiences" include environmental factors that undermine a child's sense of safety, stability, and attachment. There is a connection between the number of ACEs a person experiences and health issues as an adult.

- The tool for determining these adverse adult outcomes is the ACE quiz.

"Betrayal is a more subtle, twisted feeling than terror. It burns and eats, but terror stabs right through."

—Wendy Hoffman

NOTES:

HEALING STEPS

1. To start breaking a trauma bond, you first need to admit that one exists. Think about the trauma bond symptoms. Have you experienced one? Are you in one now?

_____

_____

_____

_____

_____

_____

_____

_____

_____

2. If you haven't already, read about mindfulness and learn how to start practicing it. Learning to be mindful and self-aware every day will help you heal trauma bonds and your emotional triggers. Mindfulness will also help you see where your boundaries need to be. Mindfulness is one of the keys to healing. Keep track of articles and books about mindfulness here. What have you learned about mindfulness and awareness so far?

3. Learn about negative self-talk, how to recognize it, and positively reframe it. Changing your self-talk is a major key to healing. Keep track of articles and books about stopping your negative self-talk here. What have you learned so far?

_____

_____

_____

_____

_____

_____

_____

_____

_____

4. Remember that beliefs are thoughts that have emotions attached to them. Eliminating inaccurate beliefs is a primary key to healing. Pick one of your childhood beliefs to examine. What thoughts and feelings are still connected to it? For example: "I won't ever be successful." List the feelings and thoughts that come up and write about them at length. Are they still relevant to your life today? Why or why not? Explain.

5. Make a list of everything that you will not miss about your trauma bond after it's dissolved.

_____

_____

_____

_____

_____

_____

_____

_____

_____

_____

_____

_____

6. Have you taken the ACE test? What's your score? What does this indicate to you? How do you feel about it?

_____

_____

_____

_____

_____

_____

_____

_____

_____

_____

_____

_____

_____

_____

_____

_____

_____

Chapter Fifteen
SLAMMING AND BANGING

BOOK CHAPTER REVIEW

- Narcissistic rage consists of unexpected and uncontrollable anger triggered by some type of narcissistic injury. For example, self-esteem or self-worth having been jeopardized or wounded.

- Holding a grudge vindicates a narcissist-mother's behavior and gives her reason to feel victimized.

- Sometimes rages are passive-aggressive; for example, sulking, giving backhanded compliments, procrastination, making sarcastic comments, withdrawal, sabotage, undermining, and using the silent treatment.

"The more you love yourself, the less nonsense you'll tolerate."

—*Unknown*

NOTES:

HEALING STEPS

1. Use the chapter's list of the triggers that could result in narcissistic rage. Write about the tantrums you've witnessed.

_____

_____

_____

_____

_____

_____

_____

_____

_____

_____

2. Write about how you handled these rages. How did they make you feel?

3. Develop a list of actions you can take to protect yourself from or to avoid a narcissistic rage.

_____

_____

_____

_____

_____

_____

_____

_____

_____

_____

_____

4. Think about how you've handled rages in the past. How might you deal with them from now on? Write your plan:

Chapter Sixteen

GASLIGHTING: THE MOST SIGNIFICANT CAUSE OF C-PTSD

BOOK CHAPTER REVIEW

- Gaslighting is a type of emotional abuse that's hard to recognize and challenging to heal.

- Gaslighting gives a narcissist a considerable amount of power and control. It's emotional abuse in the form of mind games. When narcissists gaslight, they feel superior in their control over your beliefs, feelings, thoughts, and perceptions.

- If you're frequently gaslighted, you may doubt your reality and/or your memory. You may convince yourself that your mother's version of reality is accurate.

- If the gaslighting is constant, your sense of reality may eventually depend on your mother's interpretation. You may begin to lose your sense of self.

- There are three ways we can eliminate cognitive dissonance: change our thoughts, change our actions, or justify our perceptions.

- Cognitive distortions are errors in thinking. They're a way to spin life experiences into something different than what they are, in effect, validating and maintaining a negative view of life.

"Because of its insidious nature, gaslighting is one form of emotional abuse that is hard to recognize and even more challenging to break free from. Part of that is because the narcissist exploits one of our greatest fears—the fear of being alone."

—Angie Atkinson

NOTES:

1. Start letting go. It's time to stop focusing on your mother's narcissistic behavior and start moving forward into a new way of experiencing life. It's time to start adjusting your attitude and putting yourself on your own "to-do" list as a priority. Make a conscious decision to move forward. How will you start?

2. Reclaim your personal power, self-confidence, and self-esteem. Get into counseling, take a class, learn a new skill, start a hobby. What's your plan to start working on your self-confidence and self-esteem? Set a start-date and outline your plan here:

_____

_____

_____

_____

_____

_____

_____

_____

_____

_____

3. Start building new, healthy relationships, and connect to others in new ways. Doing these will help you attract better relationships and authentic, supportive friends. Outline your plan here:

4. Gaslighting erodes your trust in yourself, so it's essential to give yourself permission to make mistakes and learn from them. Life is about attaining progress, not perfection. Remember, you're a human being. No one is perfect, regardless of what your mother may insist on. Write your thoughts about these statements here.

_____

_____

_____

_____

_____

_____

_____

_____

_____

_____

_____

_____

_____

_____

5. Continue actively exploring how your childhood and identity might have been affected by gaslighting. Write your discoveries and insights here:

6. Write about any gaslighting episodes you remember. Write how the incident occurred as you remember it, and then write how it was rewritten by your mother. If you can, find someone who was present during the original event and see how their memory of what happened compares to yours. Seek validation that your memories are accurate.

_____

_____

_____

_____

_____

_____

_____

_____

_____

_____

_____

_____

Chapter Seventeen
CODEPENDENCY

BOOK CHAPTER REVIEW

- Codependency has been defined as "a disease of a lost self," and a result of an individual's prolonged exposure to, and practice of, a set of oppressive rules which prevent the open expression of emotions and problems.

- Codependency exists on a continuum, from mild to severe, just as narcissism does. There are three stages along the continuum.

- To feel emotionally and physically safe, it becomes necessary for the child of a narcissistic mother to be hypervigilant and to control outcomes related to the mother's behavior.

- Codependency eventually affects one's ability to have healthy, mutually satisfying adult relationships.

"Not my circus, not my clowns."

—Anonymous

NOTES:

1. Write a letter to your mother that you will never send her. Tell her how she made you feel while you were growing up. Be specific. Let yourself experience any emotions that arise. Don't explain or defend her behavior. Acknowledge that you were a child and had no control over her behavior. Acknowledge that her actions, thoughts, and mental instability are not your fault; you didn't cause them, and you can't cure them.

2. In your letter, tell her how you feel about her. Describe how your life and relationships have been affected by your childhood.

_____

_____

_____

_____

_____

_____

_____

_____

_____

_____

_____

_____

_____

_____

_____

_____

_____

_____

_____

_____

_____

3. Ask yourself these questions:

- Do you feel responsible for solving other people's problems?

- Do you feel responsible for people who really aren't your responsibility?

- Do you often know how to solve other people's problems?

- Do you frequently offer unsolicited advice?

- Does it bother or hurt you when others don't take your advice?

- Do you do things for others even when they haven't asked you to?

- Do you sometimes feel resentment for helping others?

- Do you think of yourself as a "fixer" or problem-solver?

- Do you get most of your satisfaction from helping others fix their lives or solve their problems?

- Are you attracted to people based on their potential?

- Do you desire to help your romantic partner reach his or her potential?

- Do you need to be needed?

- Do you try to control outcomes so you'll feel emotionally or physically safe?

- Are you attracted to needy or emotionally unavailable people?

- Do you believe you must be in a romantic relationship to be worthwhile?

- Do you find ways to control other's behavior?

- Is it important to be liked by everyone?

- Have you risked your own safety to keep someone else safe?

- Do you monitor what's going on with others to see what you can do for them?

- Can you listen to someone talk about their problems without offering advice or trying to fix it?

- Do you save others from the consequences of their actions?

- Do you repeat yourself or over-explain, so there's no chance of being misunderstood?

- Do you often feel emotionally exhausted?

- Do people seem ungrateful for the things you do for them?

4. Answering yes to any of these indicates codependent coping skills. What have you discovered about yourself regarding codependency!?

Write your insights here:

_____

_____

_____

_____

_____

_____

_____

_____

_____

_____

_____

_____

_____

_____

_____

_____

_____

_____

_____

_____

_____

_____

_____

_____

_____

_____

_____

_____

_____

_____

_____

5. Ask yourself these questions about your current relationships, and write your insights:

- What am I minimizing?

_____

_____

_____

_____

_____

_____

_____

- What am I tolerating?

_____

_____

_____

_____

_____

_____

_____

- What am I denying?

6. Acknowledge what your body, mind, and feelings are telling you about your relationships. Again, this is a way to validate yourself because what you think and feel matters!

_____

_____

_____

_____

_____

_____

_____

_____

_____

_____

_____

7. Are you spending time trying to help and fix others? How can you practice mindfulness regarding how you spend your time?

_____

_____

_____

_____

_____

_____

_____

_____

_____

_____

_____

_____

_____

8. "Allow others the dignity and the space to make and learn from their own mistakes." How do you feel about this statement?

Chapter Eighteen

TALKING WITH YOUR NARCISSISTIC MOTHER

BOOK CHAPTER REVIEW

- You can talk with your narcissistic mother without getting hurt or frustrated, or at least minimize the severity of those.

- Narcissists have a self-centered perspective. As their emotions change, their reality changes along with it. They view the present moment in whatever way their emotional filters are presenting it.

- Narcissistic moms enjoy having pointless arguments. It's entertaining for them and is a source of narcissistic supply. She gets rejuvenated while you become drained.

- To minimize the possibility of a time-wasting, emotionally exhausting discussion, particular actions need to be taken before, during, and after talking with your narcissistic mother.

You won't have a heart-to-heart connection with your mother, but you can learn how to interact with her successfully."

NOTES:

Healing Steps

1. How does talking with or spending time with your mother make you feel?

_____

_____

_____

_____

_____

_____

2. Does your mother routinely use words that negatively affect or hurt you? Write about that here:

_____

_____

_____

_____

_____

_____

_____

3. Does your mother compliment you? Smile at you? Does she seem genuinely happy to see you? Write about your insights and feelings here:

_____

_____

_____

_____

_____

_____

4. Does she affirm or validate your thoughts and feelings? Write about your observations here:

5. Can you have a conversation with your mother without it becoming an argument or a debate?

_____

_____

_____

_____

_____

_____

_____

_____

_____

_____

_____

_____

_____

6. Begin to experiment with assertively expressing your needs and using the statements from the Gray Rock technique. Outline your plan here:

7. Does your mother always have to be right? Write about how that makes you feel:

_____

_____

_____

_____

_____

_____

_____

_____

_____

_____

_____

_____

_____

8. Do you feel comfortable saying no or disagreeing with her? Write about that here:

9. Have you felt the need to manipulate events or people to make sure they didn't witness your mother's behavior? What behaviors bother or embarrass you most?

_____

_____

_____

_____

_____

_____

_____

_____

_____

_____

_____

_____

_____

10. Do you limit the amount of time you spend with your mother because you're concerned she'll embarrass, confuse or hurt you? Explain:

_____

_____

_____

_____

_____

_____

_____

11. Do you limit or restrict topics of conversation because they may upset her or cause her to become argumentative or defensive? Explain:

_____

_____

_____

_____

_____

_____

_____

_____

12. Do you feel emotionally tired after spending time with her? Why?

_____

_____

_____

_____

_____

_____

_____

13. Would you rather avoid talking with or sending time with your mother, if you could? What would you do instead? This is telling. Try to do more of whatever you indicate here.

14. Do you feel a sense of guilt after talking with your mother? Explain why.

_____

_____

_____

_____

_____

_____

_____

_____

_____

_____

_____

_____

_____

15. Do you feel the need to "debrief" with a trusted person after spending time with or talking with your mom?

16. Do you interact with your mom from a sense of obligation rather than a genuine desire?

_____

_____

_____

_____

_____

_____

_____

_____

_____

_____

_____

_____

_____

_____

Chapter Nineteen
ADDRESSING C-PTSD

BOOK CHAPTER REVIEW

- PTSD symptoms are stress-related coping mechanisms called triggers.

- Triggers are stored memory fragments of traumatic events, and they alert us to recurring danger or threats. Our triggers signify wounds that still need to heal.

- C-PTSD results from a series of traumatic occurrences or a single prolonged traumatic event. People who have C-PTSD experience the symptoms of PTSD, but also suffer additional symptoms.

- The effects that traumatic childhoods have on adult behavior and relationships have been well documented.

- It's common to repeat the first relational patterns and attachment styles we learned as children.

"Common symptoms of C-PTSD are flashbacks, panic attacks, nightmares, excessive startle reaction, and routinely thinking about the traumatic event."

—McCllelland and Gilyard

NOTES:

HEALING STEPS

1. Continue taking steps to identify your triggers:

_____

_____

_____

_____

_____

_____

2. Deepen your practice of mindfulness to become aware of each trigger and when or where it appears. What have you learned about your triggers?

_____

_____

_____

_____

_____

_____

_____

3. Give some thought to how each trigger may have formed and how it protected you. Write about that.

_____

_____

_____

_____

_____

_____

_____

4. Think of more ways to respond to each trigger rather than letting it take over your emotional response appropriately.

_____

_____

_____

_____

_____

_____

_____

_____

5. List some of the negative messages you heard as a child.

_____

_____

_____

_____

_____

_____

_____

_____

6. Think about whether these are accurate now and whether they were ever true. Write your insights:

_____

_____

_____

_____

_____

_____

_____

_____

7. Karyl McBride, Ph.D. states that "specialized recovery involves cleaning up trauma first and accepting that your parent is not going to change. The change will be within you" (McBride, 2013). Actively recovering from trauma includes three essential pieces:

- Understanding the problem's background, history, and diagnosis.

- Dealing with feelings associated with that background and history.

- Reframing the past to change your current world-perspective.

How do you feel about these statements? Do you agree? Why or why not?

Chapter Twenty

SETTING PERSONAL BOUNDARIES

Book Chapter Review

- Setting healthy personal boundaries is the first step in healing from codependency. It is a form of self-care; boundaries protect and empower us.

- A healthy boundary gives your mother the ability to make choices, including breaking the boundary and experiencing the consequences.

- When we're healing from codependency, it's essential to start saying what we mean and meaning what we say.

- Setting boundaries is a way of affirming your authentic self and demonstrating integrity.

- Setting a boundary requires three steps.

- You do not need your mother's permission, validation, or recognition to set boundaries for yourself.

Boundaries work both ways: you will no longer violate others' boundaries by rescuing, or trying to fix them or their circumstances.

NOTES:

1. Set a boundary. Here's the first step: Identify a need (or want) you have that is not being met. (For example, you need to feel emotionally and physically safe around your mother.) Write an "I" statement, for example: "I need (or I want) to feel emotionally safe when I'm around my mother." Do that here:

2. Which of your mother's behaviors keep this need unmet? (For example, she loses her temper and throws objects.) This is the behavior that you will no longer tolerate. She will have the choice to do this thing or not, and if she does, its where you'll extend the consequences. What does she do that you are no longer willing to tolerate? Pick one thing. If there are several, write a separate boundary for each of them.

_____

_____

_____

_____

_____

_____

_____

_____

_____

3. Now figure out what will happen when she chooses to do this behavior. This will be the consequence. Write that consequence here: (For example, you will leave her presence and do something else.)

4. Now put them all three together here: (For example, "I need to feel emotionally safe when I'm with my mother. When she loses her temper and yells and screams at me, it makes me feel unsafe and afraid. I will no longer tolerate her raising her voice at me. When she begins to do that, I will leave."

_____

_____

_____

_____

_____

_____

_____

_____

_____

_____

_____

_____

5. We don't negotiate our boundaries with our mother. You're an adult, and no one can determine your boundaries but you. Only you know what's best for you. By setting a boundary, you're choosing to stay in your personal space, and not control others, or take responsibility for the outcome.

6. Ask yourself:

- Does this boundary take care of me? Or am I trying to control my mother?

- Does this boundary offer several choices? Your boundary should allow several choices, including the thing that you don't want her to do. If there are only two choices, then it's not a boundary; it's an ultimatum.

- You must follow through with the consequences if you want your mother to learn new ways of interacting with you. If you can't follow through with your chosen consequence, then you need to pick a different one.

YOU CAN DO HARD THINGS

7. Implementing your boundaries can be intimidating. Write your fears and concerns here. Outline your plan to put your new boundary in place.

_____

_____

_____

_____

_____

_____

_____

_____

_____

_____

_____

_____

_____

_____

_____

_____

_____

Chapter Twenty-one
IDENTIFYING DANGEROUS PEOPLE

BOOK CHAPTER REVIEW

> - There is a a quick and easy proactive way called the WEB method, to identify toxic, narcissistic, or dangerous individuals.
>
> - The WEB method requires paying close attention to an individual's words, your emotions, and their behavior. Doing this can provide information as to whether the person is potentially dangerous.

"Experience is the hardest kind of teacher. It gives you the test first and the lesson afterward."

—Vernon Law

NOTES:

HEALING STEPS

1. Ongoing exercise: Identify and list people, places, and things that are healthy and useful to your life today, and those that are not. Explain your reasons.

_____

_____

_____

_____

_____

_____

_____

_____

_____

2. Use the WEB method with new people you meet, as well as those you've known for a while. Write about your insights, thoughts, and feelings.

3. Begin minimizing or breaking contact with people whom the WEB method reveals to be potentially unsafe. How do you feel about doing this? How will you start?

_____

_____

_____

_____

_____

_____

_____

_____

_____

_____

_____

_____

_____

_____

_____

_____

_____

_____

_____

_____

_____

_____

_____

_____

_____

_____

_____

Chapter Twenty-two
YOU'VE GOTTA FEEL IT TO HEAL IT

BOOK CHAPTER REVIEW

> - When we start walking the recovery path, we have no idea what we'll discover along the way, and we'll need to acknowledge and heal each of those things.
>
> - We can't put a time-frame on the progression of events that will take place, set a calendar-goal around them, or compare our progress to anyone else's.
>
> - Your healing journey is yours alone.
>
> - This self-focused and insightful time will become a forever part of your life experience, and of you.
>
> - Welcome whatever you discover

"I'm here. I'm alive. I'm grateful. I'm ready."

NOTES:

Here's a checklist of healing steps. Check off the ones you've begun or completed and highlight the ones to work on next.

1. Examine, write about, and validate your childhood memories.

2. Examine and write about your feelings about narcissism, specifically when considering your mother could be one.

3. Understand that your childhood circumstances were not your fault.

4. Awareness and understanding of at least 2 of your triggers and where they came from. Have a plan for the next time you're triggered.

5. Awareness of helping others, fixing their problems, offering advice, or removing their consequences, when they haven't asked you to do those things.

6. Experience with Narcissistic Awareness Grief, and it's impact on you. What stage are you currently in?

7. Examine whether you have been a target of projection and understand how your mother used projection to see her own unacceptable traits within you.

8. Examine whether you've witnessed the narcissistic abuse cycle in your own family. If so, which stage is the family currently?

9. Examine some of the lies you were told as a child. Which ones do you still believe? Why or why not?

10. If you have experienced the silent treatment, understand how it impacted you.

11. Examine whether your family uses the rule, "Don't Talk, Don't Trust, Don't Feel," and understand how it impacts you.

12. Examine whether you've experienced feelings of shame and when it started. Read Brene' Brown's materials on shame or vulnerability.

13. Examine whether you have been a source of narcissistic supply and how you contribute to that.

14. Examine whether you are in a trauma bond and how it's affecting you. Take steps to break the bond, such as practicing mindfulness. Mindfulness is one of the keys to healing.

15. Change your negative self-talk. That is also a major key to healing.

16. Examine and question your childhood beliefs and your thoughts and feelings connected to them.

17. Develop a list of actions you can take to protect yourself from, or avoid, a narcissistic rage.

18. Write about gaslighting episodes you remember. Seek validation that your memories are accurate

19. Allow others the dignity and space to make and learn from their mistakes.

20. Have an outline to follow for conversations with your mother.

21. Set at least one personal boundary and enforced it.

22. Use the WEB method to identify potentially dangerous people.

23. Use the HALT method to ensure your needs are being met.

24. Practice "Loving Detachment."

25. Practice excellent self-care.

Self-assessment: How are you doing so far? What's next?

_____

_____

_____

_____

_____

_____

_____

_____

_____

_____

_____

_____

_____

_____

_____

_____

_____

_____

_____

Chapter Twenty-three
WHAT NOW?

BOOK CHAPTER REVIEW

- It's OK to realize you've been shortchanged.

- It's OK to acknowledge that your childhood could have been different.

- Your adult life could have been very different, too, if your mother had been emotionally stable and able to care for you properly.

- It's more than OK to feel everything you're feeling.

"Sometimes it's not "answers" that hold the key to healing, but rather it's the understanding that who we are now is the result of all our past experiences, both the good and the bad."

NOTES:

1. Write how you feel about everything you've learned up to this point. What was the most important thing you learned? What was the most helpful? What was the most shocking? What was the saddest? Which steps will you take next? Which will be the hardest? Why?

_____

_____

_____

_____

_____

_____

_____

_____

_____

_____

_____

_____

_____

_____

_____

_____

_____

_____

_____

_____

_____

_____

_____

_____

Chapter Twenty-four

A NEW BEGINNING

Once you begin to heal, you'll notice changes in your thinking, perception, and emotions. The order in which the changes occur is irrelevant, and the changes are entirely unique to each recovering individual. You'll start healing where and when you need to, on your own exclusive timetable.

Those of us who've been affected by maternal narcissism need to heal and reclaim our emotional balance, sense of self, and well-being. To recover, we must go through each stage of NAG, eliminate codependency, and set healthy boundaries.

Use this checklist to validate your healing successes.

INDICATORS OF RECOVERY:

- You're beginning to respect yourself.

- You've set some new boundaries.

- You focus more on what makes you happy and what's important to you rather than making others happy or knowing what's important to them.

- You've found activities that you love, and you do them regularly.

- You're in touch with your intuition, and you're learning to trust it.

- You realize it's not your job, and it never was your job, to treat or fix your mother or anyone else.

- You've examined your childhood programming, questioned each of the misperceptions you were expected to believe about yourself, and are working on letting go of your mother's faulty perceptions of you.

- You're creating new ideas about who you are, based on how far you've come and who you are today.

- When you see narcissistic behavior, you recognize it for what it is, and you steer clear.

- You're learning to fulfill your own needs, and you don't feel guilty about it.

- You recognize that your mother has a problem with thinking and perceiving and that she'll probably never address it.

- You understand that the crazy-making feelings you had around your mother were a normal reaction to her abnormal behavior. Your brain was functioning precisely the way it was supposed to, to protect and help you try to make sense of a situation that would never make sense.

- You're aware of when you're self-gaslighting, and you stop as soon as you become aware.

- You feel grounded and safe most of the time.

- You're getting comfortable having difficult conversations.

- You're getting comfortable confronting people who need to be confronted.

- You stand up for yourself, calmly and confidently.

- You are fiercely on your own side.

- A person's character and integrity matter more to you than their popularity, sense of humor, success, or physical attributes.

- You're not interested in continuing people-pleasing behaviors.

- You like yourself much of the time.

- You're aware of your self-talk, and make sure that it's positive.

- You focus more often on what makes you happy and what is important to you.

- You're developing personal values.

- You're working through your anger.

- You're working on forgiveness.

- You're learning to allow others to earn your trust.

- You notice when "red flags" are present. When it's not possible to avoid those individuals, you maintain low-contact and enforce your boundaries.

- You're doing recovery work on a regular basis and acknowledging your progress.

- You believe that you're a strong person.

- You're educating yourself about narcissism, toxic people, and toxic relationships.

- You're creating new beliefs about yourself based on who you've become and who you are becoming.

- You've begun to prioritize self-care in its many forms.

- You seek out and practice guided meditations that help you feel positive, strong, and peaceful.

- You journal.

- You no longer consent to people or events that intrude on your plans, privacy, safety, or serenity.

- You don't worry whether your life choices will make your mother angry or upset. You're making life choices that are all about you now.

- When a narcissist invites you to an argument, you decline. ☺

- You're aware of relationships that take advantage of you.

- You focus on solutions, not problems.

- You're more concerned about your life than anyone else's.

- You no longer tolerate people who devalue or disrespect you. You kick them out of your life, and you feel good about doing it.

- You're becoming your own advocate.

- You're beginning to know what's good for you and what isn't.

- You're no longer willing to accept someone else's version of reality.

- You're not willing to minimize your education, talents, skills, or abilities in order to accommodate someone else's personal insecurities.

- You're not willing to minimize your education, talents, skills, or abilities in order to accommodate someone else's faulty perception of you.

- You know when you're being manipulated by guilt, shame, passive-aggressive behavior, and other forms of control, and you no longer let yourself be controlled.

- You're getting comfortable with communicating about the things that you will and won't accept and/or do in your relationships.

- You recognize when you're being gaslighted and refuse to let your reality be re-written by someone else.

- You'll absolutely leave situations that make you feel uncomfortable or unsafe.

- You feel worthy of being seen and heard.

- You're uncomfortable when you're in denial, and you recognize it for what it is.

- You recognize that you are a complete person, and you don't need validation or acceptance from anyone except yourself.

- You don't need permission to exist.

- You're no longer interested in being a people-pleaser, and you understand and accept that this kind of enabling behavior makes you a potential victim.

- You refuse to give up your own plans or dreams to achieve somebody else's.

- You refuse to spend your precious time doing things you don't want to do that might gain someone's attention, affection, approval, or love.

- You've decided to stop over-functioning.

- You've decided to stop "rowing the boat" all by yourself. You understand and believe that others need to do their share of the work.

- You say "no" more often and set limits for others' behavior and expectations.

- You understand that there are consequences for every action, and you let others deal with their own consequences.

- You recognize that all relationships are two-way interactions.

- You no longer make excuses for or minimize someone else's behavior.

- You don't tolerate "walking on eggshells."

- You empathize, but you draw the line at being taken advantage of.

- You realize that boundaries work two ways: you no longer violate others' boundaries by rescuing, or trying to fix them or their circumstances.

- You ask for clarification when you're confused by something someone says or does.

- You're getting comfortable disengaging from toxic people, and you know when and why it's necessary.

- You recognize that people who use mind-games, manipulation, secrecy, intimidation, hurtful sarcasm or teasing, are toxic individuals, and you enforce the boundaries that protect you.

- You see that praise, flattery, compliments, or charm can be subtle forms of manipulation, and those simply don't work on you anymore.

- You're not willing to stay in a relationship that makes you feel drained, confused, or doubtful of your sanity or your self-worth.

- You don't tolerate others crossing your personal boundaries or talking about: your appearance, weight, relationships, or achievements.

- You accept yourself in all your imperfection.

- You understand that "perfection" doesn't exist, and that your vulnerabilities, strengths, and weaknesses all combine to create the complete and lovable person you are.

- You trust your decision-making abilities, and you make decisions more easily.

* * *

1. Where have you made progress?

_____

_____

_____

_____

_____

_____

_____

2. Where do you need to continue improving?

_____

_____

_____

_____

_____

_____

_____

3. What's your plan for continuing your healing process?

_____

_____

_____

_____

_____

_____

When we are healed, we get to live above and beyond our "fabricated childhood reality."

I wish you a lifetime of healing, personal growth, and peace.

Diane

About the Author

Diane Metcalf earned her Bachelor of Arts degree in Psychology in 1982 and a Master of Science in Information Technology in 2013.

She has held Social Worker, Counselor and Program Manager Positions in the fields of Domestic Violence and Abuse, Geriatric Healthcare, Developmental Disabilities, and Reproductive Health. She is an experienced Advocate and Speaker on the topics of Domestic Violence and Abuse. She has been a guest on Lockport Community Television (LCTV), sharing her knowledge and experience regarding Domestic Abuse with the local community. She has experienced maternal narcissistic abuse throughout her life, developed coping skills and strategies, and shares those insights here.

This book is a compilation resulting from her education, knowledge, and personal insight regarding her own traumatic experiences and subsequent recovery work. She is no longer a practicing Social Worker, Counselor, Program Manager, or Advocate, nor is she or has she ever been a licensed psychologist.

Currently, Diane lives in Las Vegas, Nevada, with her husband Kim and her goofy, adorable Goldador, Abby, and her lovable, affectionate feline, Simba. She continues to write about toxic relationships and recovery on her blog, The Toolbox (http://toolbox.dianemetcalf.com/).

This book is intended for informational purposes only and is not a substitute for professional therapy.

What's Next?

Learn more about how to heal and recover from toxic relationships!

Visit:

Toxic Undo
At
DianeMetcalf.com

Sign-up for free healing tips and tools on

The Toolbox
toolbox.dianemetcalf.com

Check out what I'm currently writing:

DianeMetcalf.com

The Lemon Moms Companion Workbook—Action Steps to Understand and Survive Maternal Narcissism

is now available on Amazon.com!

Please Leave A Review!

Love this book? Don't forget to leave a review!

Every review matters a lot!

Your review helps others, and it helps make future updated versions better!

Head over to Amazon (or wherever you purchased this book) to let me know your thoughts.

Thank you very much. I appreciate you!

~Diane Metcalf

Made in the USA
Columbia, SC
28 April 2022

59627661R00059